D1450968

SHAPE YOUR OPINION

Should Kids Get Allowance?

by Janie Havemeyer

NORWOOD HOUSE PRESS

Norwood House Press
P.O. Box 316598
Chicago, Illinois 60631

For information regarding Norwood House Press, please visit our website at:
www.norwoodhousepress.com or call 866-565-2900.

PHOTO CREDITS: Cover: © Cultura Motion/Shutterstock Images; © Alohaflaminggo/Shutterstock Images, 9; © andresr/iStockphoto, 4; © asiseeit/iStockphoto, 16; © Denis Radovanovic/Shutterstock Images, 25; © DGLimages/Shutterstock Images, 7; © Dmitri Ma/Shutterstock Images, 10; © emyerson/iStockphoto, 22; © Mikhail hoboton Popov/Shutterstock Images, 19; © Monkey Business Images/Shutterstock Images, 32, 38; © Rocketclips, Inc./Shutterstock Images, 29; © Sergey Maksienko/Shutterstock Images, 15; © SerrNovik/iStockphoto, 35; © Tom Merton/iStockphoto, 37; © YinYang/iStockphoto, 12

Hardcover ISBN: 978-1-59953-934-8
Paperback ISBN: 978-1-68404-206-7

Library of Congress Cataloging-in-Publication Data

Names: Havemeyer, Janie, author.
Title: Should kids get allowance? / by Janie Havemeyer.
Description: Chicago, Illinois : Norwood House Press, [2018] | Series: Shape your opinion | Includes bibliographical references and index.
Identifiers: LCCN 2018005354 (print) | LCCN 2018003232 (ebook) | ISBN 9781684042135 (ebook) | ISBN 9781599539348 (hardcover : alk. paper) | ISBN 9781684042067 (pbk. : alk. paper)
Subjects: LCSH: Children's allowances--Juvenile literature.
Classification: LCC HQ784.S4 (print) | LCC HQ784.S4 H38 2018 (ebook) | DDC 332.0240083--dc23
LC record available at https://lccn.loc.gov/2018005354

312N—072018
Manufactured in the United States of America in North Mankato, Minnesota.

Table of Contents

Many parents give their kids an allowance every week or month.

Opinions about Allowance

1

An allowance is money a parent gives to a child. It is often given once a week. It can also be given once a month. Kids need to learn how to handle money. An allowance gives them practice.

Ways to Give Allowance

There are two main ways parents give allowance. One is when children are not expected to do anything for it. Their allowance is given to them. They do not have to do chores to earn it.

Another way is when parents make kids do chores for their allowance. If kids don't do their chores, they don't get paid. They must earn their allowance money.

What Do the Experts Say?

Experts have many opinions about allowance. Roger Young works in **finance**. He thinks an allowance is a good idea. He believes it helps kids learn about money early. He says, "Kids' money habits are formed before they get to high school."[1] He thinks parents are the best teachers.

Some experts feel an allowance that is not earned is a bad idea. Lewis Mandell studies

Experts disagree about whether an allowance should be tied to chores.

finance. He says giving a regular allowance teaches kids to think they can get free money. Mandell argues that an allowance is not the best way to teach kids about money.

Other experts think tying allowance to chores is a bad idea. They think kids should always do their chores. These experts see chores as family responsibilities. They feel kids shouldn't expect payment for doing basic chores at home.

In Favor of Allowance

Parents are the ones who decide whether to give an allowance. Some parents say an allowance teaches important lessons. These lessons are about making good money choices. Kids learn how to be smart about spending money. They learn how to save money. They learn the value of

Kids who handle money get to practice their math skills.

a dollar. Kids also get to practice their math skills. They practice being responsible. They have a chance to give their own money to **charity**. These are all good things to practice.

Some parents think kids will spend money unwisely if they are given an allowance.

Against Allowance

Other parents think giving kids money doesn't teach them the right things. They may not like giving allowance that is not earned. They may think kids will care too much about money or be greedy. Parents sometimes worry that kids will make spending mistakes.

EXPLORE THIS BOOK

In this book, three questions about allowances will be examined. *Does an allowance teach good habits? Does an allowance teach good money skills? Should an allowance be tied to chores?* Each chapter ends with a section called **Let's Look at the Opinions**. This section focuses on points to remember when forming an opinion. At the end of the book, students can test their skills at writing their own opinion essays.

Learning to save money is a good habit for kids to develop.

2

Does an Allowance Teach Good Habits?

Yes: An Allowance Teaches Good Habits

An allowance helps kids build good habits. Kids must decide how to spend their money. They have to learn to spend it wisely. It takes time to save money to buy things. Kids learn how to wait. Waiting for something you want can be hard. But practicing how to do it is a good habit. When kids save their own money, they practice sticking with a task. They practice not giving up. They can also be **generous** by giving money away. These are all good habits.

Learning to Wait

Ron Lieber wrote a book about money. He came up with seven habits kids should learn. One habit is learning to wait. Lieber says many things happen quickly these days. There are on-demand movies. The computer gives instant information. Food can be heated quickly in the microwave. But it takes a long time to save money. Kids have to learn how to wait to buy

Kids are used to an instant response when they use a computer.

something. They feel good when they've saved enough. He says an allowance helps kids practice these skills.

Donating time and money can help kids learn to be generous.

Generosity

Lieber thinks another good habit is being
generous. He says an allowance helps kids

practice this. They can give money to a charity they like. They may support an animal shelter or a local library. Lieber believes kids are happier when they give things.

No: An Allowance Can Lead to Bad Habits

Some people are against giving kids money on a regular basis. They say this doesn't teach good habits. Instead, it causes problems. Parents worry their kids will be spoiled. They worry their kids won't learn the value of work.

Work and Rewards

Lewis Mandell studies kids and allowance. He is against giving kids an allowance without requiring work. He says these kids may not think work is important. They will be less likely to get jobs as teens. Kids need to learn that work brings rewards.

Studying Allowance

Professors at the University of Minnesota did a study on kids and money. They talked to kids who get allowances. Many of the kids wished they had more money. Many also did not think getting a job was important. The professors found that allowance can make it harder for kids to learn the value of hard work.

Some experts think kids should work for their allowance, not have it handed it to them.

3

Does an Allowance Teach Good Money Skills?

Yes: An Allowance Teaches Good Money Skills

Knowing how to use money is important. It is an important skill for everyone to learn. An allowance is one way for kids to practice. When kids have their own money, they learn many skills. They practice planning. They become smarter about spending. They learn how to save. This knowledge helps them become "money smart."

A Four-Jar System

Neale Godfrey worked as a banker. She thinks kids are growing up without money skills. She started a company. Her company helps parents with money questions. She says kids "must have real money of their own to manage."[2] That way they can practice using it. One way to practice using money is to receive an allowance.

Godfrey came up with an allowance program. Each week, kids split their allowance into four jars. One jar contains money for charity. Another holds spending money. The last two jars are for **savings**. One is to save for things kids want to buy soon. The other is to save for things kids want to buy later. That money is referred to as **long-term savings**.

Parents can help kids learn about managing money by modeling good money skills.

issue. Jumpstart talked to kids about their allowance. The kids took tests on how well they handled money.

Some kids did not receive an allowance. They got the best scores on the test. Other kids got an allowance but had to do chores for it. They scored a bit lower. The last group of kids got an allowance but did not have to work for it. They got the lowest scores.

Lewis Mandell explained the results. Kids who got a free allowance knew the least about saving and spending. Giving kids free money doesn't work. It doesn't help kids learn.

Summing It Up!

An allowance is a way for kids to get money. When kids have their own money, they can practice managing it. They can learn money skills. But they need help if this is to happen. An allowance by itself does not teach skills. Kids should talk about money with their parents. This is true whether or not kids receive an allowance.

Let's Look at the Opinions
BACK UP YOUR OPINION

It is important to give reasons for your opinion. One way to back up your reasons is with poll results. Polls show what a group of people think about a certain subject. Here two polls were used. T. Rowe Price did a poll. It said kids who handle their own money have better money habits. This shows that an allowance helps kids learn about money. Jumpstart also did a poll. It said kids with an allowance do not know more about spending and saving. This suggests an allowance doesn't teach kids about money. Using polls is a good way to back up your reasons. It is a good way to support your opinion.

Some parents require kids to earn their allowance by doing chores, such as doing the laundry.

4

Should an Allowance Be Tied to Chores?

Yes: Allowance Should Be Tied to Chores

Allowance is a good way to get kids to do chores. Kids need money to buy things they want. They can earn it by doing chores. An allowance with chores teaches kids important lessons. One lesson is that getting money means working for it. Sometimes the work is hard. It will not be fun to do. But allowance is the reward. This is true in the real world. People work for money. Doing chores and getting paid prepares kids for real-life work.

An Expert Weighs In

Neale Godfrey has written books about money. She believes kids should do chores for their allowance. She says the chores should be the same each week. Kids can dust the house. They can take out the garbage. They can change the cat litter. The number of chores depends on how old the kids are. Once all the chores are done, the kids get paid. This is their allowance. She says, "Parents do not owe their children spending money. An allowance is money that a child earns by being a working, **contributing** member of a family."[3]

Kids can do many household jobs to help the family.

What about Parents?

Most parents want their kids to do chores for allowance. In 2015, a finance company talked to families. It asked them about allowances. Did kids have to do chores for their allowance?

Eighty-five percent of the families said yes. Many parents think paying for chores is good training. Working for pay helps kids prepare for the future. Kids will grow up and get jobs. They will earn money by working.

No: Allowance Should Not Be Tied to Chores

Some people think kids should not have to do chores for their allowance. Housework is not something they should get paid for. Adults do not get paid to do housework. So why should kids? Chores are a kid's duty to his or her family. Everyone in the family should help around the house. Allowance should not be the reward for being helpful.

Some experts say kids should not be paid to help with household chores such as setting the table.

Allowance Is Not a Salary

Joline Godfrey teaches families about money. She says an allowance is not a salary. A salary is money a person earns at a job. She says, "Do not tie an allowance to performing tasks that should be part of family life."[4]

Parents sometimes pay kids for doing extra jobs at home on top of their basic chores.

Step Two: *Find out more.*

Before you write, find out more about your subject. Read what other people have to say. You could look up poll results on the subject. Ask other people what they think, especially if they know a lot about a subject. Find out the facts. See if an expert has something to say on the subject.

Step Three: *State your opinion.*

The first few sentences should say what your paper is about. You may want to include a question. For example, you could start this way: "This essay is about allowance. It asks the question, Is an allowance good for kids?"

Next, write down your opinion. You can use phrases such as *I think, I believe,* or *in my opinion.* Examples are:

- I think an allowance is good for kids.
- I believe an allowance helps kids learn about money.
- In my opinion, an allowance should not be tied to chores.

Step Four: *Give reasons.*

Opinions should be followed up with reasons for those opinions. Logical reasons can influence others to think like you. Come up with two or three reasons why you think the way you do about your subject. Write each reason in a sentence. Use linking words like *because, since,* and *therefore* to connect your opinion with the reasons why you came to a certain conclusion. For example, if you are writing a piece on whether students should or should not get an allowance, you might give these reasons:

- I think kids should not get an allowance without doing chores, *since* this will not teach them the value of work.
- I think kids should get an allowance *because* it will help them learn money skills.

Step Five: *Support your reasons.*

The opinion of a famous person or an authority is a good way to back up your reason. So are results from a survey or research study. Here is an example of how to do this:

First, give an opinion with a reason:

- I think kids should get an allowance *because* they need to practice using and saving money.

Then, give a fact to back up the reason:

- One expert agrees. He said getting an allowance lets kids practice waiting to buy the things they want.

Step Six: *Write the ending.*

Summarize your opinion in the last sentence or two. This makes it clear for the reader what side you are on and why you think the way you do. A good summary wraps up your argument and helps convince the reader to think as you do. You could begin the last sentence with any of these phrases, or you can think of your own:

- For all these reasons, . . .
- As the survey results indicate, . . .
- To sum up, . . .

GLOSSARY

budgeting (BUHJ-it-ing): Planning how to spend and save money so it doesn't run out.

charity (CHAIR-ih-tee): An organization that helps people in need.

contributing (cun-TRIB-yoo-ting): Helping out.

finance (FY-nance): The business of managing money.

generous (JEN-er-us): Freely giving and sharing with others.

long-term savings (LAWNG-turm SAY-vings): Money that is set aside to be used much later.

savings (SAY-vings): Money that is put somewhere safe so it can be used later.

BIBLIOGRAPHY

Books

Brennan, Linda Crotta. *Managing Money.* Mankato, MN: The Child's World, 2013.

Furgang, Kathy. *Everything Money.* Washington, DC: National Geographic, 2013.

Kemper, Bitsy. *Budgeting, Spending, and Saving.* Minneapolis, MN: Lerner, 2015.

Websites

The Mint: Fun for Kids
www.themint.org/kids/

Money Games for Kids
dfi.wa.gov/financial-education/games-kids

SOURCE NOTES

1. T. Rowe Price Group, Inc. "T. Rowe Price: Parents Are Likely to Pass Down Good and Bad Financial Habits to Their Kids." *Cision.* PR Newswire. 23 Mar. 2017. Web. 18 Mar. 2018.

2. Neale S. Godfrey. *Money Doesn't Grow on Trees: A Parent's Guide to Raising Financially Responsible Children.* New York: Simon & Schuster, 2006. Print. 23.

3. Ibid., 30.

4. Joline Godfrey. *Raising Financially Fit Kids.* Berkeley, CA: Ten Speed Press, 2013. Print. 49.

Index

About the Author

Janie Havemeyer is an author of many books for children. She is a graduate of Middlebury College and Bank Street College of Education. For many years, Janie taught in elementary schools and in art museums.